CELEBRATING THE FAMILY NAME OF HAMILTON

Celebrating the Family Name of Hamilton

Walter the Educator

Silent King Books
a WhichHead Entertainment Imprint

Copyright © 2024 by Walter the Educator

All rights reserved. No part of this book may be reproduced in any manner whatsoever without written permission except in the case of brief quotations embodied in critical articles and reviews.

First Printing, 2024

Disclaimer

This book is a literary work; the story is not about specific persons, locations, situations, and/or circumstances unless mentioned in a historical context. Any resemblance to real persons, locations, situations, and/or circumstances is coincidental. This book is for entertainment and informational purposes only. The author and publisher offer this information without warranties expressed or implied. No matter the grounds, neither the author nor the publisher will be accountable for any losses, injuries, or other damages caused by the reader's use of this book. The use of this book acknowledges an understanding and acceptance of this disclaimer.

Celebrating the Family Name of Hamilton is a memory book that belongs to the Celebrating Family Name Book Series by Walter the Educator. Collect them all and more books at WaltertheEducator.com

USE THE EXTRA SPACE TO DOCUMENT YOUR FAMILY MEMORIES THROUGHOUT THE YEARS

HAMILTON

The name Hamilton, bold and grand,

Celebrating the Family Name of

Hamilton

A legacy that shapes the land.

From ancient hills to bustling streets,

The Hamiltons' story proudly beats.

In every corner of the earth,

Their name is known, it speaks of worth.

Of wisdom gained, of battles fought,

Of dreams pursued and victories sought.

From highland winds that whisper low,

To city lights that fiercely glow,

The Hamiltons have carved their path,

With strength and courage in their wrath.

Builders of bridges, creators of dreams,

They see the world through vibrant streams.

Their vision broad, their purpose clear,

With every step, they persevere.

Celebrating the Family Name of

Hamilton

They rise like dawn with steady hands,

To shape the seas and till the lands.

With every breath, they push ahead,

Their hearts alive, their spirits fed.

From leaders bold to scholars bright,

The Hamiltons stand for what is right.

They move with grace, they speak with fire,

And lift the world with their desire.

Through every trial, through every turn,

The Hamiltons' hearts forever burn.

A flame that guides them through the dark,

A spark of hope, a steadfast mark.

With minds that soar and eyes that see,

The Hamiltons craft their destiny.

They lead with honor, walk with pride,

Celebrating the Family Name of

Hamilton

With truth and justice at their side.

From castles old to city towers,

They've built a legacy that flowers.

In every generation born,

The Hamiltons' strength will not be worn.

For in their name, a story's told,

Of hearts so brave, of spirits bold.

A family tied by bonds so deep,

A promise that they always keep.

ABOUT THE CREATOR

Walter the Educator is one of the pseudonyms for Walter Anderson. Formally educated in Chemistry, Business, and Education, he is an educator, an author, a diverse entrepreneur, and he is the son of a disabled war veteran. "Walter the Educator" shares his time between educating and creating. He holds interests and owns several creative projects that entertain, enlighten, enhance, and educate, hoping to inspire and motivate you. Follow, find new works, and stay up to date with Walter the Educator™

at WaltertheEducator.com

www.ingramcontent.com/pod-product-compliance
Lightning Source LLC
LaVergne TN
LVHW012051070526
838201LV00082B/3909